CREATE POSITIVE HABITS

BY SUSANNE M. BUSHMAN

BLUE OWL BOOKS

TIPS FOR CAREGIVERS

Social and emotional learning (SEL) helps children manage emotions, learn how to feel empathy, create and achieve goals, and make good decisions. Strong lessons and support in SEL will help children establish positive habits in communication, cooperation, and decision-making. By incorporating SEL in early reading, children will be better equipped to build confidence and foster positive peer networks.

BEFORE READING

Talk to the reader about forming habits. Explain that habits are part of our everyday lives.

Discuss: What are habits that you have? Have you formed a new habit recently? How did you do it? What are habits you'd like to form?

AFTER READING

Talk to the reader about different habits he or she could start.

Discuss: What is a small habit you want to form? What is a big goal that you could use habits to help with? What would the cue for your habit be? What would the reward for your habit be?

SEL GOAL

Self-awareness is a crucial part of discovering what habits we already have, both positive and negative. Self-monitoring is an effective and efficient way for kids to see the habits of their lives. Help readers monitor their actions for a few days to a week. They could keep journals or use other methods to keep track. At the end of the tracking period, help readers look for and identify habits. What are good habits they have? What are habits they want to change? How will they work to change them and create new ones?

TABLE OF CONTENTS

CHAPTER 1

HEALTHY HABITS

Do you brush your teeth every night? Do you wash your hands before eating? Maybe you always drink water with meals. These are healthy **habits**!

Habits are activities you do regularly.
You don't need to think hard about them.
They are part of your daily **routine**.
Maybe you walk your dog every day!

Sometimes we want to make new and better habits. This can be hard! But it is worth it. Positive habits make us happier and healthier.

Habits help us meet **goals**, too. Maybe your goal is to score more points in basketball. So you create a habit. You practice every evening before dinner.

BE KIND

Being kind can be a habit, too! Thank your bus driver. Smile. Lend your friend a helping hand. Kindness can brighten someone's day!

CHAPTER 2

FORMING HABITS

Start slow. Maybe you want to start a new **hobby**. At first, you practice twice a week. Then you add one day each week. Soon, you practice every day!

Break down big habits into small actions. Maybe you want to read more this summer. You can't start by reading 10 books in one day. You start by reading one chapter each day.

When should you do habits?
After a cue! Cues tell us to do
our habits. For many people,
getting in the car is a cue.
It tells us to put our seat
belts on. Time can be a cue.
Maybe you get ready for bed
at eight o'clock.

Actions can be cues, too. You finish
breakfast. Then you help clear
the table. Even people can
be cues! When you see your
grandpa, you smile!

Rewards help, too. You do your homework every day when you get home. Then you play outside or on your tablet. These things **motivate** you.

Rewards help form habits. But sometimes you stop needing them! The habit becomes part of your routine. You do it even without a reward.

tablet

CHAPTER 3

MINDFUL HABITS

Make healthy habits for your mind. Like what? Make it a habit to **reflect**. Write or draw in a journal each night. Do a self-check. How does your body feel? What **emotions** do you feel?

journal

When we reflect, we build **self-awareness**. This helps you understand your feelings! It can help you see habits you might want to stop, too. Maybe you always fight with your brother before school. It puts you in a bad mood.

We can break bad habits by forming new, positive habits. Maybe you **focus** on bad parts of your day. You worry they will happen again. Try making **gratitude** a habit. Each day at dinner, share something you are grateful for.

WAKE UP RIGHT

Morning is a great time for positive habits! Start your morning off right. Clear your mind. Eat a good breakfast. Prepare for the day ahead! Say three good things you will do today.

Practicing **mindfulness** is another positive habit! Mindful thinking focuses on the present. It helps us relax and enjoy the moment. Try **meditating**. Or just focus on your breathing.

BODY SCAN

A body scan is one way to be mindful. Find a comfortable spot. Close your eyes. Then think about your toes. What do they feel? Slowly think about each part of your body, moving up from your toes.

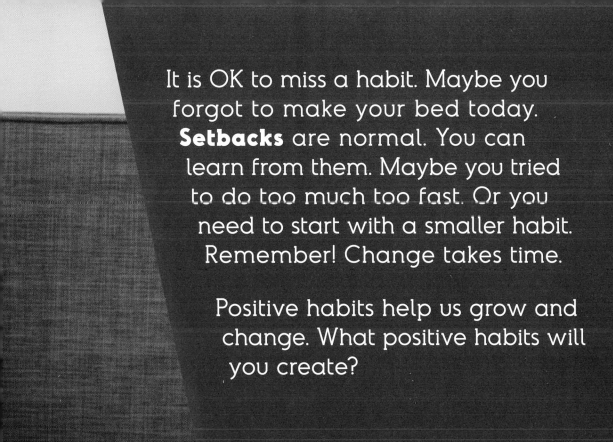

It is OK to miss a habit. Maybe you forgot to make your bed today. **Setbacks** are normal. You can learn from them. Maybe you tried to do too much too fast. Or you need to start with a smaller habit. Remember! Change takes time.

Positive habits help us grow and change. What positive habits will you create?

GOALS AND TOOLS

GROW WITH GOALS

Habits can be hard to form! There are different things you can do to make forming habits easier.

Goal: Create a positive habits chart! Write your habits down one side of the piece of paper. Then write the days of the week along the top. Put a sticker or draw a star for each day of the week you do one of your positive habits!

Goal: Identify meaningful rewards. What motivates you? Identify the things that will be most effective in rewarding you when you do your habit.

Goal: Identify people who can help you form habits. Having a support network can make habit forming easier!

MINDFULNESS EXERCISE

Mindfulness is a great habit! Try this exercise to get started.

1. Find a comfortable spot to sit.

2. Close your eyes.

3. Take deep breaths. Focus on your breathing.

4. Count with your breath. One when you breath in. Two when you breath out. Go up to 10. Then start over.

5. When your mind wanders, just return to thinking about your breathing. It is natural for the mind to wander.

GLOSSARY

emotions
Feelings, such as happiness, anger, or sadness.

focus
To concentrate on something.

goals
Things that you aim to do.

gratitude
A feeling of being grateful or thankful.

habits
Activities and behaviors that you do regularly, often without thinking about them.

hobby
Something that you enjoy doing when you have free time.

meditating
Thinking deeply and quietly as a way of relaxing your mind and body.

mindfulness
A mentality achieved by focusing on the present moment and calmly recognizing and accepting your feelings, thoughts, and sensations.

motivate
To encourage someone to do something or want to do something.

reflect
To think carefully or seriously about something.

rewards
Things that you receive in recognition of your efforts or achievements.

routine
A regular sequence of actions or way of doing things.

self-awareness
The ability to recognize your own emotions and behaviors.

setbacks
Problems that delay you or keep you from making progress.

TO LEARN MORE

FACT SURFER

Finding more information is as easy as 1, 2, 3.

1. Go to www.factsurfer.com

2. Enter "**createpositivehabits**" into the search box.

3. Choose your cover to see a list of websites.

INDEX

Blue Owl Books are published by Jump!, 5357 Penn Avenue South, Minneapolis, MN 55419, www.jumplibrary.com

Library of Congress Cataloging-in-Publication Data is available at www.loc.gov or upon request from the publisher.

ISBN: 978-1-64527-199-4 (hardcover)
ISBN: 978-1-64527-200-7 (paperback)
ISBN: 978-1-64527-201-4 (ebook)

Editor: Jenna Trnka
Designer: Molly Ballanger

Photo Credits: princessdlaf/iStock, cover; Mahathir Mohd Yasin/Shutterstock, 1; DougSchneiderPhoto/iStock, 3; somethingway/iStock, 4; SerrNovik/iStock, 5; monkeybusinessimages/iStock, 6–7, 16–17; jmsilva/iStock, 8; Africa Studio/Shutterstock, 9, 15 (background), 23; Monkey Business Images/Shutterstock, 10–11; imtmphoto/Shutterstock, 12–13; ParkerDeen/iStock, 14; Darrin Henry/Shutterstock, 15 (foreground); Aaron Amat/Shutterstock, 18–19; kate_sept2004/iStock, 20–21.

Printed in the United States of America at Corporate Graphics in North Mankato, Minnesota.